What Are
Sleep Disorders?

Other titles in the *Understanding Mental Disorders* series include:

What Are Sleep Disorders?

Leanne Currie-McGhee

ReferencePoint
Press®

San Diego, CA

© 2016 ReferencePoint Press, Inc.
Printed in the United States

For more information, contact:
ReferencePoint Press, Inc.
PO Box 27779
San Diego, CA 92198
www.ReferencePointPress.com

LIBRARY OF CONGRESS CATALOGING-IN-PUBLICATION DATA

Currie-McGhee, L. K. (Leanne K.)
  What are sleep disorders? / by Leanne Currie-McGhee.
    pages cm -- (Understanding mental disorders)
  Audience: Grade 9 to 12.
  Includes bibliographical references and index.
  ISBN-13: 978-1-60152-930-5 (hardback)
  ISBN-10: 1-60152-930-9 (hardback)
 1. Sleep disorders--Juvenile literature. I. Title.
  RC547.C87 2016
  616.8'498--dc23
                                                        2015012870

CONTENTS

INTRODUCTION

Everyone Needs Sleep

Sleep. Everyone needs it. It restores the body and soul and is a necessary component of life. Unfortunately, millions of Americans do not meet their basic sleep needs. Sleep deprivation, lack of sleep, and sleep disorders—disorders that cause disruption to the normal sleep process—affect between 50 million and 70 million Americans.

Lawrence Neumann's sleep disorder caused problems not only for himself, but also for his wife. During the day, Neumann was a kind man who acted considerately and lovingly to his wife of many years, Bonnie. This all changed at night, after he fell asleep. Neumann would scream obscenities at his wife, kick his legs, punch, and violently hurl himself out of bed. On one occasion he leaped out of bed, hit his head on a nightstand, and received a large gash. Another time he threw himself out of bed headfirst and received a concussion after hitting the floorboards.

This went on for sixteen years, and neither he nor his wife, nor his local physician, knew what to do. Finally, at age seventy-one, after extensive neuropsychiatric tests and three separate sleep studies, he received a diagnosis from a neurologist at Northwestern University's Feinberg School of Medicine. Neumann had a little-known condition called REM behavior disorder, in which people unconsciously act out their dreams during sleep.

Odd Sleep Times

Unlike Neumann, Cat Mocha does not have problems when she sleeps. Instead, she cannot get to sleep during normal times. Her internal clock is disrupted, which means she cannot sleep during typical nighttime hours. Mocha has been diagnosed with delayed sleep phase disorder, which means her body does not follow a normal day-night schedule.

"What this disorder meant for me was that my natural sleep cycle was later than the average person," writes Mocha. "The perfect sleep times for me were from four am to 12 pm."[1] This disorder does not fit well for working a job with typical hours or going to school.

A Multitude of Problems

Neumann and Mocha experience two of the more than ninety different types of sleep disorders identified by the International Classification of Sleep Disorders. Some types, such as insomnia and restless leg syndrome, are common; others, such as narcolepsy and non-24 disorders, are less so.

For people who do not get enough rest, the days can feel long and difficult. Being tired throughout the day and not having energy are common effects of sleep disorders. This can significantly diminish a person's quality of life and ability to enjoy oneself. Sleep disorders can also lead to serious physical and emotional issues. "Sleep is the fuel of life," says Gayle Green, author of *Insomniac*. "It's nourishing; it's restorative. And when you are deprived of it, you are really deprived of a basic kind of sustenance."[2]

> "Sleep is the fuel of life."[2]
>
> —Gayle Green, author of *Insomniac*.

Sleep disorders can result in serious physical problems, such as high blood pressure, obesity, irregular heartbeat, and stroke. A study published in a 2011 issue of *Hypertension*, a journal of the American Heart Association, found that people who got the least amount of deep sleep were 80 percent more likely to develop high blood pressure than people who got longer, less interrupted sleep. "People should recognize that sleep, diet, and physical activity are critical to health, including heart health and optimal blood pressure control,"[3] says researcher Susan Redline. Emotional problems are also linked to sleep disorders; a 2007 study of ten thousand people found that those with insomnia were five times as likely to develop depression as those without.

Sleep deprivation can also lead to a lack of alertness that can be very dangerous. For instance, a person who does not get enough sleep is more likely to cause a car accident. The National Highway Traffic Safety Administration estimates that fatigue is a cause in 100,000

Millions of Americans do not get enough sleep every night. Some simply do not practice good sleeping habits; others suffer from sleep disorders that stem from mental, physical, or emotional problems. Uncontrolled sleep disorders can negatively impact a person's health and alertness.

auto crashes and 1,550 crash-related deaths a year in the United States. Another issue is that people can cause problems at work if they are not adequately alert. A 2012 study by researchers at Harvard Medical School found that insomnia is responsible for 274,000 US workplace accidents and errors each year.

Life Without Sleep

Fortunately, for those who suffer from disorders, there is help. Provided they are diagnosed properly, most sleep disorders have treatments that can alleviate—and in some cases eliminate—sleep problems. For Neumann, it was very relieving to get a diagnosis after years of suffering. His doctors treated him with the medication clonazepam and treated his mild case of sleep apnea, which can contribute to REM behavior disorder episodes. "It was the first time in more than 16 years that I could say I got a good night's sleep,"[4] Neumann says.

While Mocha's disorder cannot be cured, certain methods have helped her manage symptoms. She benefited from chronotherapy, which involves moving bedtime sequentially one to three hours or more later on successive nights until the desired bedtime is reached. She also tried bright light therapy, which involves exposing a person to bright light in timed spurts to reset the body's internal clock. These and other methods can help sufferers live a more normal life.

With millions of Americans in need of treatment, health professionals are putting more emphasis on sleep research. Funding for sleep research has increased over the last decade as researchers search for causes and cures. The hope is that in the coming years more people will be able to get the help they need.

"People should recognize that sleep, diet, and physical activity are critical to health, including heart health and optimal blood pressure control."[3]

—Susan Redline, professor of sleep medicine at Harvard Medical School.

CHAPTER 1

What Are Sleep Disorders?

To most people, sleep is a natural part of life. They go to bed at night and wake up in the morning, ready for the day. But those who suffer from sleep disorders feel physically and emotionally exhausted, sluggish, and anxious; are unable to focus; and have other health problems.

What exactly is a sleep disorder? According to the Cleveland Clinic, a renowned medical facility in Ohio, "Sleep disorders are conditions that prevent a person from getting restful sleep and, as a result, can cause daytime sleepiness and dysfunction."[5] Basically, if a person has trouble falling asleep, wakes up and cannot get back to sleep, or suffers from a condition that disrupts sleep, he or she has a sleep disorder. More than ninety sleep disorders have been classified to date.

Bob is one of the 40 million Americans who have a chronic, long-term sleep disorder. He suffers from sleep apnea, a disorder in which a person stops breathing while asleep. "It started insidiously enough. I felt a little more tired than usual and I began to have a little trouble concentrating," says Bob. "My memory was a little off as well. . . . At the same time, my wife began complaining that my snoring was becoming difficult to live with."[6] Bob eventually decided to see a doctor and received a diagnosis. If diagnosed, many sleep disorders have treatments that will help alleviate symptoms and help people get a good night's sleep.

How Do We Sleep?

To understand how sleep disorders interrupt the sleep process, one must know how normal sleep works. During a typical night, people experience five stages of sleep, the last of which is rapid eye movement

(REM) sleep. After a person passes through the five stages, which usually takes 90 to 110 minutes, the cycle begins again. Typically, adults spend about 50 percent of their total sleep in stage two sleep, 20 percent in stage five (REM) sleep, and the remaining 30 percent in the other phases; infants, however, spend about half their sleep in REM sleep.

Stage one is a light sleep in which a person can be awakened easily and not even realize that he or she has been asleep. During stage two, eye movements stop and brain waves become slower. Stage three is when extremely slow brain waves, called delta waves, are interspersed with smaller, faster waves. By stage four almost all of the brain waves emitted are delta waves; stages three and four, together, consist of deep sleep. Lastly, people enter REM sleep, where their breathing is more rapid, their heart rate increases, their eyes jerk back and forth, and dreams occur. To remain mentally and physically healthy, people need to experience the entire cycle about five times a night.

"Sleep disorders are conditions that prevent a person from getting restful sleep and, as a result, can cause daytime sleepiness and dysfunction."[5]

—Cleveland Clinic, a highly regarded nonprofit medical center.

How Much Sleep Is Enough?

Although every person requires a different amount of sleep, health professionals have recommended ranges for people's minimum sleep requirements. Sleep needs are affected by age, health, and gender. The National Sleep Foundation called together a panel of eighteen leading scientists and researchers to determine the latest sleep recommendations; it released these guidelines in 2015.

Newborns need between fourteen and seventeen hours of sleep to thrive and grow. When they enter infanthood, defined as four to eleven months, they need eleven to fourteen hours. Experts suggest that toddlers also get eleven to fourteen hours, which can be reduced to ten to thirteen hours once they are of preschool age. School-age children need between nine and eleven hours, which slightly decreases to eight to ten hours when they become teenagers. The sleep range for young and middle-age adults is seven to nine hours and goes down to seven to eight hours once over age sixty-five.

A person's sleep needs also depend on the totality of his or her sleep. If someone gets two hours less sleep than needed for two nights in a row, the body needs to make up the four hours by sleeping longer over the next few nights. This is because bodies need to make up for sleep debt, the difference between the amount of sleep a person should get and the amount they actually get. Doctors advise that sleep should not be seen as an indulgence or luxury but as a necessity. For good health, a person needs to "repay" his or her sleep debt. Often people who have sleep disorders have a high sleep debt that does not get repaid.

Why Is Sleep Important?

In many ways, sleep is a mystery. Scientists know our bodies require sleep to survive, but they cannot explain exactly why. Nor can they completely explain what happens when our bodies are sleeping. From what they have researched, scientists know people cannot live without sleep, and poor sleep negatively affects health.

Researchers have different theories regarding why we need sleep. One is that sleep restores the body and allows it to repair and rejuvenate itself. This theory has gained prominence in recent years with support from various studies. One study found that animals deprived entirely of sleep lose all immune function and die in just a matter of weeks. The regular life span for a rat is two to three years, but sleep-deprived rats can only survive for five weeks on average.

In 2013 scientists at the University of Rochester reported that people need sleep to clear out waste products made by their brains. These include metabolites, degradation products that brain cells secrete during regular tasks in waking hours. The body's waste is cleared out by the lymphatic system, but the brain is disconnected from that system and needs another way to rid itself of waste. The brain's waste—such as beta-amyloid, which has been associated with Alzheimer's disease—is carried out on the waves of its cerebrospinal fluid down to the liver for elimination. The study discovered that the brain's waste is removed twice as fast when sleeping, and without sleep it is difficult for the brain to clear all waste.

Sleep Needs by Age

According to the National Sleep Foundation, sleep needs vary by age. Infants require the most sleep, while adults over sixty-five require much less.

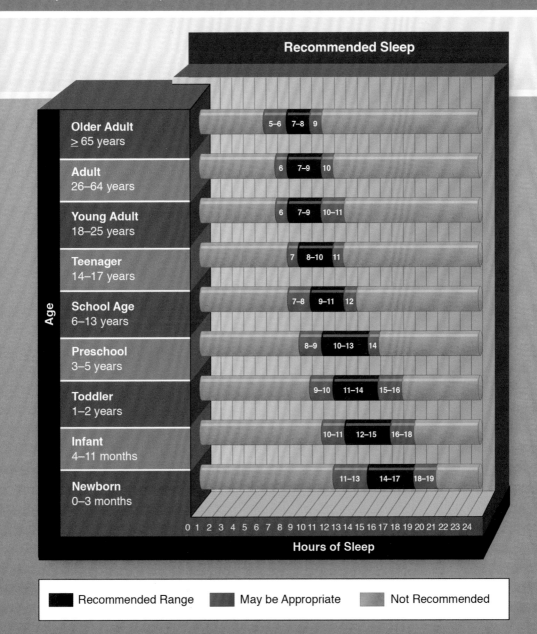

Recommended Sleep

Age		Hours of Sleep
Older Adult ≥ 65 years		5–6 / 7–8 / 9
Adult 26–64 years		6 / 7–9 / 10
Young Adult 18–25 years		6 / 7–9 / 10–11
Teenager 14–17 years		7 / 8–10 / 11
School Age 6–13 years		7–8 / 9–11 / 12
Preschool 3–5 years		8–9 / 10–13 / 14
Toddler 1–2 years		9–10 / 11–14 / 15–16
Infant 4–11 months		10–11 / 12–15 / 16–18
Newborn 0–3 months		11–13 / 14–17 / 18–19

0 1 2 3 4 5 6 7 8 9 10 11 12 13 14 15 16 17 18 19 20 21 22 23 24

Hours of Sleep

■ Recommended Range   ■ May be Appropriate   ■ Not Recommended

Source: National Sleep Foundation, "How Much Sleep Do We Really Need?," 2015. http://sleepfoundation.org.

Scientists are also aware of the consequences of not getting enough sleep, a symptom of most sleep disorders. These consequences include unclear thinking, diminished motor capability, inability to focus, and lack of coordination. According to a 2014 study by the University of Oxford, lack of sleep may affect the size of a person's brain. A total of 147 adult volunteers underwent magnetic resonance imaging (MRI) scans to determine what the link is between sleep and brain volume. The study found that sleep problems like insomnia can have an impact on a person's brain over time, causing it to shrink, and shrink more rapidly, than those without sleep problems.

Brain cells produce waste materials as they function throughout the day. The body uses sleep to hasten the rate at which the brain rids itself of this waste. Researchers conclude that limiting sleep time can lead to a buildup of these wastes, which consequently can impair normal, wakeful brain activity.

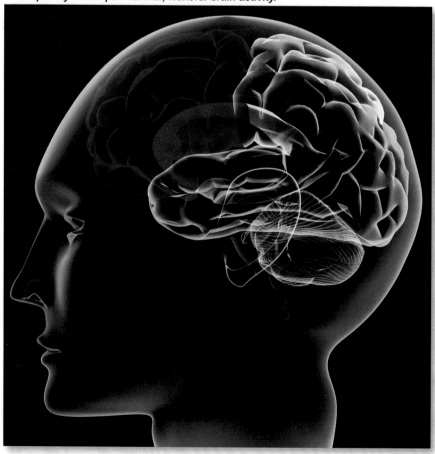

Kids Who Cannot Sleep

Adults are not the only ones who cope with sleep disorders. A National Sleep Foundation poll found that about two out of every three kids under the age of ten have experienced some type of sleep problem.

One to 3 percent of children experience sleep apnea and have difficulty breathing because of obstructed air passages. Those with narcolepsy often have their first episode as a teen. And because puberty affects a person's internal clock, teens may experience circadian sleep disorders. Another common problem is sleep terrors, in which a child screams, thrashes about, and exhibits intense fear while asleep. These are not nightmares, as children do not wake up during the experience and also do not remember it the following morning. To cope, kids and teens must get diagnosed and not have their sleep problems dismissed as normal for their age. "If left untreated, sleep problems can have a significant impact on the cognitive, social, and emotional functioning of children and adolescents," write Lisa Meltzer and Jodi Mindell, authors of *Behavioral Sleep Disorders in Children and Adolescents.*

Seth Maxon discovered this for himself at age eighteen when he toured Europe. He decided to go without sleep to see what would happen—and made it for four days—with dangerous results. "As the sleepless days passed, I experienced the increasingly severe psychological effects common with extended sleep deprivation: I hallucinated, rambled, and lost focus," Maxon writes. "Toward the end of the ordeal, in New York's John F. Kennedy Airport, my body was giving out, too. While imposing a monologue on my biology teacher—who, I later learned, thought I was tripping on LSD—I blacked out and slumped mid-sentence."[7] Maxon ended up in the hospital for a week, then spent several months recovering his ability to focus and rid himself of the anxiety that had developed.

The Most Common Sleep Disorder

Unlike Maxon, most people do not purposely deprive themselves of sleep. Instead, they suffer from a disorder over which they have no control. Of these, insomnia is the most common. In this disorder a person cannot fall asleep, or falls asleep but then wakes up and cannot get back to sleep. About 30 percent of adults experience one or more symptoms of insomnia, according to a 2007 review in the *Journal of Clinical Sleep Medicine.*

Acute insomnia is the most common type of insomnia. This is when a person experiences insomnia for a short amount of time, such as a few days to a few weeks. Acute insomnia typically occurs due to stressful life circumstances, and it can usually be resolved without any treatment. Insomnia is considered chronic when a person has it at least three nights a week for three months or longer.

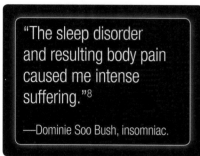

"The sleep disorder and resulting body pain caused me intense suffering."[8]

—Dominie Soo Bush, insomniac.

Insomnia is also categorized as either primary or secondary. Primary insomnia is when a person's insomnia is not directly caused by another health condition. Secondary insomnia is caused by an existing health problem such as arthritis, asthma, or a medication side effect.

Living with insomnia is difficult. About 10 percent of people experience functional impairment and distress over not sleeping, and about 6 percent experience these symptoms for at least one month, as reported by a 2007 review in the *Journal of Clinical Sleep Medicine.* People who experience insomnia generally feel dissatisfied with their sleep and have fatigue, low energy, difficulty concentrating, mood disturbances, and decreased performance at work or school.

Dominie Soo Bush suffered from chronic insomnia for years, starting at age sixteen. At one point, while in her thirties and working as a legal secretary, she functioned on just two to three hours of sleep a night. "The sleep disorder and resulting body pain caused me intense suffering," writes Bush. "I walked around like a zombie most days from the sleep deprivation, yet I had to function and pushed myself very hard just to take care of daily responsibilities."[8] She would feel sluggish all day and eventually stopped working until she was able to get her insomnia under control.

When Breathing Stops

Snoring can be annoying to others. A wife may ask a husband to roll over, irritated because she cannot sleep due to his snoring. What many do not realize is that snoring may be a symptom of one of the more serious sleep disorders—sleep apnea. Sleep apnea is when a person stops breathing for short periods of time while asleep.

There are three types of sleep apnea: obstructive, central, and mixed. Obstructive sleep apnea is caused by a physical blockage of the airway, usually when the soft tissue in the rear of the throat collapses and closes during sleep. During central sleep apnea the airway is not blocked, but the brain fails to signal the muscles to breathe. Mixed sleep apnea is a combination of the first two types. Of the three, obstructive sleep apnea is the most commonly diagnosed.

With each apnea event, the brain rouses the sleeper, usually not to full wakefulness, to signal breathing to resume. That is why people with

Obstructive sleep apnea occurs when soft tissue at the back of the throat blocks the upper airway, causing short periods in which breathing stops. The obstruction is typically caused by decreased muscle tone around the air passage or an increase in the amount of soft tissue in the area.

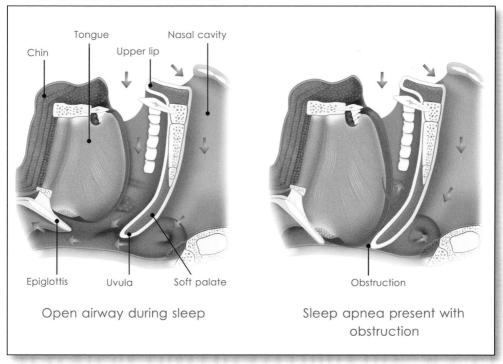

Chin — Tongue — Upper lip — Nasal cavity

Epiglottis — Uvula — Soft palate — Obstruction

Open airway during sleep

Sleep apnea present with obstruction

Some Sleep Disorders Are Temporary

Lying on a tropical beach is relaxing, but when people travel through several time zones to get there, they may find themselves tired and disoriented. This is because people's internal clocks do not adjust as quickly as they travel. This problem, called jet lag, occurs when a person crosses time zones and attempts to sleep at their regular time elsewhere. For years jet lag was considered a state of mind and not physical. Now, however, studies show that this problem is actually a temporary circadian sleep disorder. It results from an imbalance in a person's natural internal clock. When traveling to a new time zone, the body's circadian rhythms are typically slow to adjust and remain on their natural biological schedule for several days. Travelers seeking relief are advised to go out into the sunshine as much as possible during the day; avoid caffeine and alcohol, as these disrupt the sleep cycle; and take a hot bath before bedtime, as the drop in temperature when getting out of the tub encourages sleepiness.

sleep apnea experience fragmented and poor-quality sleep. Sleep apnea may lead to more serious conditions, such as high blood pressure and other cardiovascular diseases, memory problems, weight gain, impotence, and headaches.

Sleep apnea afflicts more than 18 million people in the United States, according to the American Sleep Apnea Association. The risk factors for sleep apnea include being male, overweight, and older than forty. However, sleep apnea can affect anyone, including children. The vast majority of sleep apnea patients remain undiagnosed and therefore untreated.

Restless Legs

After a long day, most people crawl into bed, allow their bodies to relax, and then fall asleep. For those with restless legs syndrome (RLS), however, bedtime is when their legs start to throb and move involuntarily, which keeps them up or wakes them later if they do manage to fall asleep. RLS is diagnosed when a person feels throbbing, pulling, creeping, or other unpleasant sensations in the legs and has an uncontrollable urge to kick or move them in some way. This disrupts sleep by either preventing someone from falling asleep or waking him or her up.

In addition to dealing with leg pain and throbbing during inactivity, RLS patients complain of being tired and groggy during the day. Linda Ledingham developed RLS after giving birth to her first child and has dealt with it for over thirty-five years. It was ten years before she was even diagnosed. "The sensations were moving up my legs, it had now reached my thighs and sleep was ever evasive,"[9] says Ledingham. RLS can be treated, but not cured, so its sufferers often experience sleeplessness and tiredness, which affects their daily lives.

RLS is among the most common sleep disorders. The National Institutes of Health estimates that as many as 10 percent of the US population may have RLS. Studies have found that moderate to severe RLS affects about 2 to 3 percent of US adults (about 5 million people). About one-third of these adults are pregnant women. One theory for why pregnant women are affected is that RLS is tied to iron deficiency, which pregnant women are prone to because of the iron required to carry oxygen to a developing fetus. Additionally, RLS is estimated to affect about 1 million children.

> "The sensations were moving up my legs, it had now reached my thighs and sleep was ever evasive."[9]
>
> —Linda Ledingham, restless legs syndrome sufferer.

Sleep Attacks

Millions of people are afflicted with many of the less common sleep disorders. One of these is narcolepsy. Narcolepsy is a neurological disorder that causes people to experience excessive daytime sleepiness and intermittent, uncontrollable episodes of sleep during the day. These sleep attacks occur suddenly, with little or no warning. People with narcolepsy do not sleep like others. Instead of experiencing the first four sleep stages, they go into the REM phase almost immediately after falling asleep.

About one in two thousand people in the United States are affected by narcolepsy, according to the Narcolepsy Network. However, it estimates that only about 25 percent of those suffering from narcolepsy actually get diagnosed and receive treatment. Narcolepsy is often combined with cataplexy, a symptom in which a person deals with sudden loss of muscle tone that leads to weakness and loss of voluntary muscle control. Cataplexy occurs in about 70 percent of all people with narcolepsy.

Aside from the dangers associated with poor sleep, narcolepsy sufferers are at risk for accidents that can stem from their sudden sleep attacks. Amanda Vasas started experiencing narcolepsy symptoms at age sixteen and eventually had to leave school and be tutored at home due to her episodes. "I started passing out up to five times a day," Vasas writes of her first symptoms. "I would be in the middle of a conversation, or walking to the bathroom, or watching TV and just fall over, completely dead weight, and be unknown to the world for about three minutes."[10] She felt immense relief after getting diagnosed; even though there is no cure for narcolepsy, she understood what was happening to her and could seek treatment for it.

> "I would be in the middle of a conversation, or walking to the bathroom, or watching TV and just fall over, completely dead weight, and be unknown to the world for about three minutes."[10]
>
> —Amanda Vasas, narcoleptic.

Living Their Dreams

Many sleep disorder sufferers actually live their dreams instead of just seeing them. People with REM behavior disorder (RBD) act out their dreams in their sleep. They may kick, punch, jump, walk, run, or talk in their sleep, which may cause them to hurt themselves or others near them.

During REM sleep people normally experience muscular atonia, a temporary paralysis. RBD, however, is caused by a dysfunction of the brain stem mechanisms responsible for the normal suppression of muscle tone and paralysis in REM sleep. People with this disorder do not undergo this paralysis and thus experience their dreams very actively. RBD is a fairly new sleep disorder, as it was not classified until 1986.

RBD is relatively rare and affects less than 1 percent of the population. Typically, those who experience RBD are male and older than fifty, although there are women and even children who have been diagnosed. According to the website Medical News Today, of all cases studied, 90 percent occur in males, and the average age is sixty years. Also, many who have RBD are afflicted with Parkinson's disease. In some cases the Parkinson's disease occurs first; in others, the RBD is first. Researchers continue to study the link between the two.

Day or Night?

Some people have no trouble falling and staying asleep, but they struggle with sleeping at a normal time. People with circadian rhythm disorders experience neurological disorders in which the sleep-wake cycle is out of sync with the day-night cycle. Internal body clocks—groups of nerve cells in the brain called the suprachiasmatic nucleus—regulate a person's circadian rhythms, the patterns that cause humans to feel sleepy at nighttime and awake during the day. Most people's circadian rhythms occur over an approximately twenty-four-hour cycle. People with circadian rhythm disorders have internal clocks that do not function correctly, which affects their circadian rhythms. This means they cannot fall asleep at typical times and are awake at odd times, which makes it difficult to function.

The most common types of circadian rhythm disorder include delayed sleep phase disorder (DSPD) and non-24-hour sleep-wake disorder (non-24). DSPD is when people cannot fall asleep until very late at night and, subsequently, need to sleep until late morning or early afternoon to achieve full sleep. Non-24 is a condition in which a person's internal clock has a day length significantly longer than twenty-four hours. This means he or she will naturally fall asleep later and later with each day, never remaining on a set schedule.

More youth and young adults are affected by DSPD than older adults. According to the American Academy of Sleep Medicine, DSPD is seen in 7 to 16 percent of adolescents and young adults. Non-24 is common in totally blind people because they do not see light, which normally regulates the twenty-four-hour day-night cycle. Because both of these disorders are often misdiagnosed as insomnia, it is unknown how many people are actually affected by them.

From adolescence until early adulthood, Oijo Baphuacs could not follow a twenty-four-hour wake-sleep cycle without becoming chronically exhausted and sick. "My college years were made extremely difficult by chronic fatigue: e.g., falling asleep in class and failing to sleep at night," Baphuacs recalls. "I felt heavy and exhausted nearly all of the time, as if my body were fundamentally 'confused.'"[11] Graduate school was easier for him because he did not have to follow a set schedule, and afterward he accepted a job that allowed him to keep a schedule that was set around his disorder. Realizing that at some point he would need to follow a typical schedule, Baphuacs spent many years researching ways he could sleep more normally so his days would not result in exhaustion.

Baphuacs is one of the many people who have benefited from a proper diagnosis. A person who feels chronically tired and does not sleep well is very likely being affected by one of the more than ninety sleep disorders that have been discovered to date.

CHAPTER 2

What Causes Sleep Disorders?

What happens when we sleep, why we need sleep, and what prevents us from sleeping is not entirely understood. But with sleep disorders so common, researchers and doctors are actively researching what causes them. Medical professionals have made progress in more effectively diagnosing sleep disorders, determining what causes them, and identifying the risk factors of developing them.

In 1993 the US Department of Health and Human Services founded the National Center on Sleep Disorders Research. The job of health researchers there and at other medical facilities around the world is to determine whether there are specific risk factors for each disorder and what causes them. Additionally, they investigate the adverse effects of each sleep disorder and the potential cures and treatments.

To date, health professionals have determined that there are general risk factors for all sleep disorders and specific risk factors for each individual sleep disorder. The same is true for health dangers that can result from the disorders. By understanding the causes, risk factors, and dangers, the hope is that the medical community can better prevent, diagnose, treat, and, in some cases, cure the sleep disorders that affect millions.

Diagnosing a Sleep Disorder

The first step to understanding a person's sleep problems is to diagnose which disorder they have. Once this is known, doctors can determine what may have caused the disorder and what can be done to treat it. The problem is that many people who suffer from sleep disorders are undiagnosed. Indeed, the National Institutes of Health estimates that about 95 percent of people who have a sleep disorder remain undiagnosed.

To get diagnosed, people must see a doctor. They are then usually asked to keep a sleep log for several weeks to identify their sleep habits. The typical sleep log contains how many hours a person sleeps each night, how often he or she wakes up and for how long, how long it takes to fall asleep, when he or she falls asleep and wakes up, how well rested the person feels upon waking, and how sleepy he or she feels throughout the day.

Sleep logs are one of the most useful tools in diagnosing a circadian sleep disorder. The sleep log of a person with a circadian sleep disorder will show a pattern of sleep disruption caused by a mismatch between a person's circadian sleep-wake pattern and the pattern required by that person's environment. If a person's sleep log shows that he consistently falls asleep late at night even when attempting earlier sleep, the person likely has a circadian sleep disorder.

A Trip to the Sleep Lab

Physicians use sleep logs and other tests to determine if more extensive studies are needed. If so, the next step is to go to a sleep lab and undergo a polysomnography (PSG). Electrodes and other monitors are placed on the patient's scalp, face, chest, limbs, and finger. These devices measure brain activity, eye movement, muscle activity, heart rate and rhythm, blood pressure, and how much air moves in and out of the lungs while a person sleeps. This test also determines the amount of oxygen in the patient's blood. A PSG is painless and just requires a person to sleep at the sleep lab while being monitored.

Technicians may record a video of the patient during the PSG. This is done when doctors suspect a person to have REM behavior disorder (RBD). The video will show excessive body movements during REM sleep, which is a symptom of RBD, as opposed to temporary muscle paralysis that normally occurs.

Erin Fuchs decided to undergo a sleep study after experiencing extreme sleepiness during the day and frequent nighttime awakenings that were often triggered by the fact that she would shout while experiencing vivid dreams. Fuchs spent thirty hours at the New York University Sleep Center, during which time she was hooked up to

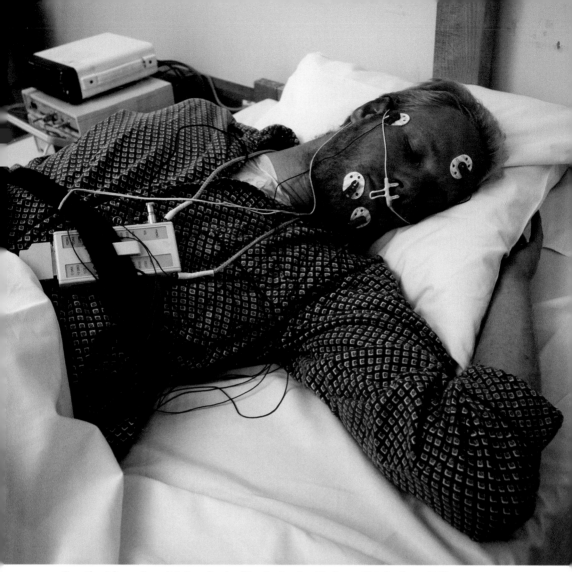

A patient in a sleep lab is wired with electrodes that monitor brain activity, breathing, heart rate, and other body functions. The data acquired from the monitors can help doctors diagnose symptoms of sleep disorders and develop effective treatments.

electrodes—small round conductors that were placed on her face and scalp to send electrical signals of her brain and muscle activity to measuring equipment—and told to sleep as she normally would. "I had to wait for the tech to come back a little after 10 p.m. to hook me up to a few more wires and connect some of them to a monitor next to the bed," remembers Fuchs. "I couldn't move, so the tech had to cover me with two blankets, which made me feel like a small child being tucked in."[12] She woke up on and off throughout the night.

Because Fuchs experienced excessive daytime sleepiness (EDS), she also was given the Multiple Sleep Latency Test. This tests for EDS by measuring how quickly a patient falls asleep in a quiet environment. It is similar to the PSG, but it is conducted during the day. During daytime naps, an electroencephalograph is used to measure and record brain wave activity while an electrocardiograph records heart rate and rhythm. A person's breathing, oxygen levels, muscle tone, and eye and extremity movements are also monitored.

Fuchs was diagnosed with idiopathic hypersomnia, a rare sleep disorder in which a person experiences severe sleepiness during the day. What makes idiopathic hypersomnia different from other sleep disorders that cause EDS is that none of the usual causes of EDS are present. An idiopathic hypersomniac's nighttime sleep is not interrupted from movement or breathing problems, and the person's internal clock is normal. Even though the person's nighttime sleep is not disrupted, he or she still never feels rested.

Other Diagnostic Tools

Individual disorders have diagnostics specific to them. Restless legs syndrome (RLS), for example, is diagnosed differently than most sleep disorders. This is because the problem has more to do with movement of the legs and not a person's ability to get to or stay asleep. To diagnose RLS, doctors have four basic criteria that they check

Cell Phones Disrupt Teen Sleep

Teenagers who excessively use their cell phone are more prone to disrupted sleep, restlessness, stress, and fatigue, according to research presented at the 2008 annual meeting of the Associated Professional Sleep Societies. One reason for this, according to a 2010 Pew Research study, is that 84 percent of teenagers sleep with, next to, or even holding their cell phones. Teens admitted that they often text during the night or wake up to texts and calls. The result is disrupted sleep, which causes daytime tiredness, less alertness, and poor performance at school.

with their patient: whether symptoms are worse at night and absent or minimal in the morning; if a person has a strong and overwhelming urge to move his or her limbs; if the urge to move is triggered by rest, relaxation, or sleep; and if a person feels relief if he or she moves the affected limb. If these criteria are met, the person is diagnosed with RLS.

Narcolepsy also involves a unique test. Narcoleptics can be tested for the level of hypocretin, a chemical that helps promote wakefulness, in the fluid that surrounds their spinal cord. To get a sample, a spinal tap procedure is conducted in which a doctor inserts a needle into the lower back area and withdraws a sample. A person with narcolepsy will have a lower level of hypocretin than normal.

In addition to a sleep study, people at risk for sleep apnea may undergo an oximetry test. Oximetry is the measure of oxygen in the blood, and abnormal drops in oxygen levels at night indicate a person is not breathing properly while sleeping. An overnight oximetry test can be done at home with a device clipped to a person's finger while he or she sleeps. The data in the device can be output into a graph showing the person's oxygen levels throughout the night, which informs the diagnosis.

Common Risk Factors

Since the 1920s, when Dr. Nathaniel Kleitman (now known as "the father of American sleep research") began studying sleep and circadian rhythms, researchers have achieved a greater understanding of sleep and have determined some common risk factors for all sleep disorders. One factor is age. About half of all adults over the age of sixty-five have some sort of sleep disorder. As people age they are more likely to have a chronic medical illness, such as heart disease, that interferes with sleep. Older people are also typically less active during the day, perhaps due to being retired or in poorer health, and activity level can affect the ability to sleep. The elderly are also more likely to be on medications that can cause sleep issues.

Medical conditions such as fibromyalgia and multiple sclerosis are also linked to sleep disorders. According to the National Fibromyalgia Research Association, more than 75 percent of people with fibromyalgia, a musculoskeletal disorder, complain of sleep disturbances and daytime fatigue. In 2014 researchers at the University of California, Davis, surveyed more than twenty-three hundred individuals with multiple sclerosis, a degenerative disease that involves the nerves, and found that more than 70 percent screened positive for one or more sleep disorders. Because of other symptoms, sleep disorders in people with these conditions often go undiagnosed. For example, fatigue is a common symptom of multiple sclerosis, but it is also a symptom of a sleep disorder; to determine if the fatigue is a result of multiple sclerosis or a sleep disorder requires further investigation by a doctor.

Several other life situations are linked to sleep disorders. Women undergoing menopause, people working night shifts, and patients taking certain medications are all more susceptible to sleep disorders. Knowing that they have certain factors that heighten their risk can help people with sleep issues pursue a diagnosis.

The Causes of Insomnia

Each sleep disorder has specific risk factors and causes. Specific causes of insomnia, for example, can be lifestyle-related, such as drinking too much alcohol and/or caffeine. The immediate effect of alcohol is to make a person fall asleep more quickly, but it later disrupts a person's REM sleep; the more alcohol one has, the more disrupted sleep he or she experiences. Caffeine, on the other hand, is a stimulant that keeps a person awake.

> "Stress causes insomnia by making it difficult to fall asleep and to stay asleep, and by affecting the quality of your sleep."[13]
>
> —Neil B. Kavey, director of the Columbia Presbyterian Sleep Disorders Center.

Another factor that affects insomnia is stress. According to Neil B. Kavey, director of the Columbia Presbyterian Sleep Disorders Center, "Stress causes insomnia by making it difficult to fall asleep and to stay asleep, and by affecting the quality of your sleep. Stress causes hyperarousal, which can upset the balance between sleep and wakefulness."[13]

Gender matters too, as women are more likely than men to develop insomnia. A National Sleep Foundation poll showed that 63 percent of women report having insomnia several nights a week,

Insomnia Affects More Women than Men

According to the National Sleep Foundation, women have more trouble falling and staying asleep than men. One reason women have trouble falling and staying asleep is likely due to changing hormones during pregnancy, their normal menstruation cycles, and menopause.

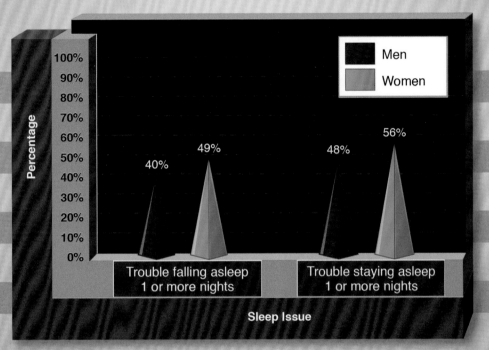

Men vs. Women Sleep Issues

Source: National Sleep Foundation, "Lack of Sleep Is Affecting Americans, Finds the National Sleep Foundation," December 2014. http://sleepfoundation.org.

compared to 54 percent of men. Contributing factors are that women are more prone to sleep issues during pregnancy and menopause.

People with insomnia may have developed the disorder due to a neurological cause. Recent research has also found that insomnia is more prevalent in people who have brains that exhibit a higher level of neuron activity and whose motor cortex—the part of the brain where nerve pulses originate—exhibits a greater ability to learn new actions. In 2014 researchers at Johns Hopkins University focused on the motor cortex, which is located at the back of the frontal lobe. They found that in insomniacs, the motor cortex had increased plasticity (the ability to change and learn) and more excitability among neurons in this region. "Insomnia is not a nighttime disorder," says study leader Rachel E. Salas, an assistant professor of neurology. "It's a 24-hour brain condition, like a light switch that is always on. Our research adds information about differences in the brain associated with it."[14]

Genetics may also cause insomnia. Research suggests that genes that control the sleep-wake system play a role in childhood insomnia. A 2014 University of Pennsylvania study of twins, for example, found that genetic factors contributed to 33 to 38 percent of insomnia cases among participants who were on average eight to ten years old. Insomnia's heritability—that is, the observed differences in a trait among individuals of a population that are due to genetic differences—was 14 to 24 percent when the average age of participants was fourteen to fifteen years old. Researchers say that molecular genetic studies are needed to specifically identify which genes are causing the heritability and to understand why the heritability decreases as the person ages.

> "Insomnia is not a nighttime disorder. It's a 24-hour brain condition."[14]
>
> —Rachel E. Salas, assistant professor of neurology.

The Causes of Sleep Apnea

Being male, over age fifty, and/or overweight puts a person at the highest risk for developing sleep apnea. For reasons not yet understood, African Americans are at the highest risk of developing this sleep disorder, though all races, genders, and ages can develop it (particularly if overweight). Being overweight can cause the extra fat tissue to thicken the wall of the windpipe, which narrows its inside and makes it harder to keep open.

In 2014 a study by the University of Pennsylvania Medical Center found that having a fat tongue may also increase the risk for sleep apnea. The study included ninety obese adults with sleep apnea and

At-Home Testing

Do you think you could sleep with people watching you? It's not an easy task, particularly for someone with a sleep disorder. A polysomnograph at a sleep lab is supposed to examine a person's sleep, but the presence of other people and machines can make it hard for a patient to sleep well enough to be monitored. It is also an expensive test: it typically costs $900 to $2,000 and may not be covered by health insurance. As a result, home polysomnograms, which cost $300 to $600, have been developed and are now accepted by many sleep doctors and are preferred by many health insurance companies over a sleep lab study.

All at-home sleep test devices measure information related to breathing and blood oxygen level. A person self-attaches sensors, which collect information while he or she sleeps. Although at-home devices are less expensive and more comfortable for patients, their accuracy is questionable: technical failures occur in as many as 20 percent of such tests. Despite this fault, at-home sleep tests are becoming the norm for diagnosing many patients.

ninety obese adults without it. The participants with sleep apnea had significantly larger tongues, tongue fat, and percentage of tongue fat (tongue fat compared to total tongue size) than those without sleep apnea. The researchers believe that the higher levels of tongue fat may prevent muscles that attach the tongue to bone from positioning the tongue away from the airway during sleep. "Tongue size is one of the physical features that should be evaluated by a physician when screening obese patients to determine their risk for obstructive sleep apnea,"[15] says American Academy of Sleep Medicine president Timothy Morgenthaler.

The Need to Move

The causes of RLS are unknown, but research indicates there may be a genetic factor. The disorder often runs in families, with 40 to 90 percent of affected individuals reporting that they have at least one first-degree relative (mother, father, or sibling) with RLS. Studies also suggest that the early-onset form of the disorder is more likely to run in families than the late-onset form.

Genetic factors are not the only indicators of an increased risk of RLS. For example, people with other disorders—such as life-threatening kidney failure called end-stage renal disease, diabetes mellitus, multiple sclerosis, rheumatoid arthritis, and Parkinson's disease—are at greater risk of developing the condition. Additionally, people with low iron levels and pregnant women are also more likely to develop RLS.

Many studies indicate that RLS is related to an iron deficiency in certain parts of the brain. Iron is a part of many critical brain cell activities, including producing a chemical messenger called dopamine. One of dopamine's functions is to signal triggers to the nervous system that help the brain control physical movement. Researchers believe that the dopamine system may malfunction, causing the abnormal movements. They also believe the iron deficiency is linked to this malfunction, but they are unclear as to how.

One of the latest investigations into what causes RLS was conducted at the Johns Hopkins University School of Medicine and was published in 2013. This study used MRI scans of the brain and found that glutamate, a neurotransmitter involved in arousal, appears abnormally high in people with RLS. The more glutamate the researchers found in the thalamus—the part of the brain involved with the regulation of consciousness, sleep, and alertness—the worse these people sleep. High levels of glutamate can result from a diet too high in gluten (found in any food that has wheat) and casein (a protein in dairy products); eliminating such foods can help reduce the levels. There are also pharmaceuticals that can reduce glutamate levels in the brain, but they have not been offered as a first-line treatment for RLS patients. More studies supporting this finding may change that, however.

Diagnosing Narcolepsy

Like many sleep disorders, narcolepsy's exact causes are unknown. In 2000, however, research found that those with narcolepsy have low levels of hypocretin, the chemical that helps promote wakefulness. In 2013 University of California, Los Angeles, researchers made

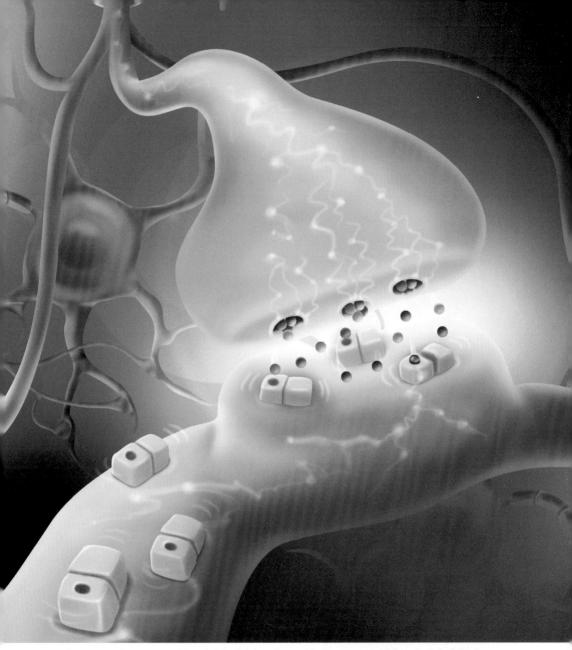

Glutamate (represented by pink balls) is released by one neuron (above) and picked up by receptors on a neighboring neuron (below), creating an electrical current. A study from Johns Hopkins University noted high levels of glutamate in the brains of patients who suffer from restless legs syndrome.

progress in determining what may cause low levels of hypocretin. The team found higher numbers of a particular brain cell type that contains histamine, which is a chemical that works as part of the immune system to kill invading cells.

In the study, people with narcolepsy had an average of 64 percent more histamine neurons than non-narcoleptics, which led researchers to theorize that histamine may be attacking hypocretin cells. Researchers have not determined what causes the histamine cells to attack, but they believe that people with narcolepsy may suffer from an issue that causes their immune system to malfunction. This knowledge eventually could lead to better treatment or even a cure.

Narcolepsy also has a genetic component. A variation of the HLA-DQB1 gene called HLA-DQB1*06:02, which is part of a family of genes called the human leukocyte antigen complex, has been strongly associated with narcolepsy. In particular, people who have cataplexy in addition to narcolepsy are found to have this gene variation. These genes are present in people with narcolepsy, but researchers are not yet sure how much of a factor they are in the development of narcolepsy.

REM Behavior Disorder

RBD is another sleep disorder in which the cause is usually unknown. For 55 percent of people with RBD, the cause is unknown; for the other 45 percent, the cause is associated with withdrawal from alcohol or sedatives. Risk factors include being male and older than sixty.

RBD is also linked to various degenerative neurological conditions, such as Parkinson's disease, multisystem atrophy, diffuse Lewy body dementia, and Shy-Drager syndrome. RBD often precedes the development of these neurodegenerative diseases by several years. In one study, 38 percent of patients diagnosed with RBD subsequently developed Parkinson's disease. Also, RBD is seen in 69 percent of those with Parkinson's disease and multisystem atrophy. Although researchers have found a connection, they do not yet understand how RBD is exactly related to these diseases. "There's a link between RBD and Parkinson's," says Aleksandar Videnovic, a neurologist at Northwestern Memorial Hospital, "but it's unclear [what it is]. Some believe that RBD is an early manifestation of Parkinson's, but much more research is needed in this area."[16]

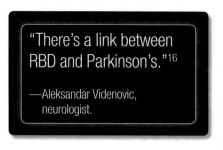

"There's a link between RBD and Parkinson's."[16]

—Aleksandar Videnovic, neurologist.

The Causes of Circadian Sleep Disorders

Medical professionals believe an inadequate ability to reset the sleep-wake cycle in response to environmental time cues, such as day and night, is the cause of circadian sleep disorders. An individual's circadian, or internal, clock might have an unusually long cycle and/or might not be sensitive enough to time cues. It is unclear, however, why these circadian clock differences occur.

A 2014 University of Missouri study was conducted to better understand the internal clock. The researchers discovered that a protein called REV-ERB plays an important part in regulating mammals' internal clocks. The researchers tested how compounds that target this protein affect circadian rhythm. In their study, the team tested a synthetic drug-like molecule called SR9011 on mice with dysfunctional circadian rhythms that possessed anxious behavior. This molecule, the researchers say, activated the REV-ERB protein and restored the rats' wakefulness while reducing anxiety, leading to a hope that this can someday be done in people troubled by circadian sleep disorders.

This is one of the many studies that have been undertaken to better understand the causes, risk factors, and dangers of sleep disorders. Understanding the hows and whys of sleep disorders is essential to better treating and eventually curing them.

CHAPTER 3

What Is It Like to Live with a Sleep Disorder?

Doctors say that sleep is as essential for a healthy life as nutrition and exercise. But sleep disorders rob millions of Americans of the opportunity to live well and feel good. "There is strong evidence that sufficient shortening or disturbance of the sleep process compromises mood, performance and alertness and can result in injury or death," say researchers Michael H. Bonnet and Donna L. Arand. "In this light, the most common-sense 'do no injury' medical advice would be to avoid sleep deprivation."[17]

Sleep disorders not only make daily life unpleasant, but they also can severely impact a person's physical and mental health and his or her performance at work or school. Living with a sleep disorder is difficult, tiring, and at times nearly impossible.

The Ability to Focus

A universal consequence of having a sleep disorder is feeling drowsy and tired throughout the day. According to J.F. Pagel of the Rocky Mountain Sleep Disorders Center, about 20 percent of adults in the United States report a level of daytime sleepiness that interferes with daily activities. According to Michael J. Breus, a clinical psychologist with the American Board of Sleep, a person's daytime alertness can be reduced by as much as 32 percent with just one and a half hours less sleep than normal. This leads to focus and attention problems that have severe, even lethal, consequences.

Indeed, lack of alertness can cause accidents when drivers fail to pay attention or even fall asleep at the wheel. The National Highway Traffic Safety Administration estimates that drowsy driving is responsible for at least 100,000 automobile crashes, 71,000 injuries, and 1,550 fatalities each year. "A drowsy driver on the road can look a lot like a drunk driver," says Justin McNaull of AAA, a roadside-assistance service organization. "They have trouble keeping their car between the lines. Speed will vary."[18] According to the National Transportation Safety Board, up to 52 percent of single-vehicle crashes in which heavy trucks are involved are fatigue-related accidents.

Driving While Drowsy

Too little sleep can be dangerous—especially on the road. A survey of more than ninety-two thousand adults found that those who sleep less than five hours per night are nearly four times more likely to fall asleep behind the wheel than those who get eight hours of sleep.

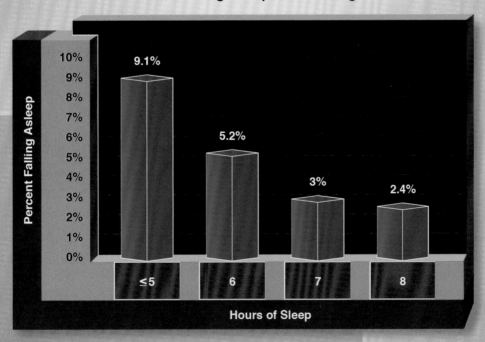

Percent Falling Asleep While Driving

Source: *MMWR Weekly*, "Drowsy Driving and Risk Behaviors—10 States and Puerto Rico, 2011–2012," July 4, 2014. www.cdc.gov.

Memory and Cognitive Ability

Sleep disorders also impact memory and cognitive ability. In 2003 neurologists at the University of Pennsylvania forced people to stay awake for eighty-eight hours—three consecutive nights—and also had people experience chronic sleep loss, sleeping only four to six hours a night for fourteen consecutive nights. Memory and simple math tests were part of the way subjects were tested on their cognitive ability. In both cases the cognitive abilities of the sleep-deprived individuals were seriously impaired. One test checked a person's reaction time; a reaction that took longer than five hundred milliseconds was considered a lapse. In a reaction-time test, those who got enough sleep scored zero to one lapses over a ten-minute period, but those who were sleep restricted averaged up to sixteen lapses.

In 2014 another study—this one conducted by the New York University School of Medicine and the Peking University Shenzhen Graduate School—linked sleep to cognitive ability. In this study, researchers trained mice to walk on top of a rotating rod. After the mice did so, researchers used advanced microscopes to look at their brains while they slept. This allowed them to see the differences between mice that got sleep and mice that were sleep deprived. The mice that got enough sleep formed significantly more brain connections called synapses—which play a major role in creating lasting memories and improve the ability to learn—than the sleep-deprived mice. "Finding out sleep promotes new connections between neurons is new and nobody knew about this before," says Professor Wen-Bio Gan from New York University. "This is just the latest piece of science to highlight the heavy importance of a good night's sleep."[19]

In addition, sleep disorders may result in a higher risk of cognitive problems such as dementia. A 2014 sleep study conducted by the University of California, San Francisco, on a large sample of veterans found that those diagnosed with sleep disorders such as apnea or insomnia were 30 percent more likely to suffer dementia than veterans without such problems. Similarly, a University of Toronto study found that 80 to 90 percent of senior adults with REM behavior disorder (RBD) develop brain disease. The study's authors suggest that

Coast Guard Restricts Those with Sleep Disorders

In 2015 the US Coast Guard proposed new rules that would disqualify merchant mariners with narcolepsy and other severe sleeping disorders from sailing. The Coast Guard is concerned that people with these disorders could cause an accident or problem while performing their duties on the ship. Merchant mariners—sailors who export and import goods—are required to obtain sailing certification for their jobs, but the Coast Guard proposed denying certification in cases where the sailor has narcolepsy or other severe sleeping disorders.

neurodegeneration of the brain might first affect areas that control sleep before attacking areas that cause other brain diseases like Alzheimer's.

Lost Hours and Low Productivity

Sleep-deprived people lose approximately 25 to 30 percent of their ability to perform useful mental work with each twenty-four-hour period of sleep loss. They have difficulty concentrating, which leads them to make mistakes at work and not get work accomplished in a timely manner. In fact, US businesses lose approximately $63 billion a year due to lost productivity from insomnia, according to experts at Harvard Medical School. In a 2011 survey of more than seventy-four hundred workers around the country, it was found that employers lose about $2,300 per year per employee who struggles with chronic insomnia. According to the study, insomnia-related presenteeism—showing up at work but not really accomplishing anything productive—causes the average US employee to lose the equivalent of 11.3 days of work every year.

Sleep disorders can also keep a person from getting a desired job. Naturally, some jobs are difficult to perform if a person is chronically tired or at risk of falling asleep during work hours. However, the

International Association of Sheet Metal, Air, Rail, and Transportation Workers allows employees with sleep disorders to work, but only if they can prove they are receiving proper treatment. Similarly, the Federal Aviation Administration allows pilots with sleep apnea to fly, but only if their disorder is being effectively treated. On the other hand, narcolepsy is typically a disqualifying condition from enlisting in the military services, even if treated.

Despite this, companies are prohibited from not hiring someone just because they have a sleep disorder. This is because some sleep disorders may be covered under the Americans with Disabilities Act of 1990, which prohibits companies from discriminating against a person with a recognized disability. According to the statute, a person is considered disabled if he or she has a physical or mental impairment that substantially limits one or more major life activities.

To be covered, however, a person must be able to provide a record of such impairment. In other words, just having a sleep disorder does not mean a person is covered by the act; it must be proved that the disorder affects his or her life. If covered, the act requires an employer to provide reasonable accommodations, such as flexible hours or longer breaks, so the person can perform his or her duties. For example, a reasonable accommodation for a person with a circadian sleep disorder who qualifies for a disability would be to provide natural sunlight or full-spectrum lighting at his or her work space.

Relationship Problems

Sleep-deprived individuals also find that their social lives are impacted by their lack of sleep. Many feel too tired to participate in activities or to socialize. Jo Dickinson, who has for years been plagued with chronic insomnia, deals with this every day. Despite trying a variety of treatments that range from medications to cognitive behavioral therapy, she typically sleeps less than four hours a night for weeks on end. "I get fatigued and too tired to do things like go out to dinner with friends," says Dickinson. "Not because I'm afraid I'll fall asleep, but because I just can't deal with socializing and putting out the extra effort."[20]

Lack of sleep affects a person's mood and how he or she interacts with others. Rebecca Wiseman developed insomnia while pregnant, and it grew worse over the years. She averages just three hours of sleep a night, which has led to arguments with others. "I'm tired and get headaches all the time, which my doctor says is caused by my lack of sleep," explains Wiseman. "I don't have the energy that I used to, to

Difficulty falling asleep and staying asleep can take its toll on marital relationships. A University of Pittsburgh study found that it was more likely for both spouses to report communication problems the longer it took for the wife to fall asleep on the previous night.

play with my older girls, and it causes stress between my husband and me."[21]

Indeed, studies have also shown that sleep disorders can bring dysfunction to relationships. In 2011 researchers at the University of Pittsburgh found that when women experience sleep problems, it negatively impacts their marriages. The study of thirty-five couples measured the amount of time it took each partner to fall asleep, their total sleep time, and the number of times they woke up during the night. In a series of daily questionnaires, participants reported whether they had negative or positive interactions with their spouse the following day. The longer it took a woman to fall asleep, the more likely it was that both husband and wife reported negative interactions, such as feeling ignored or being criticized. "There is some evidence to show that women tend to be more communicative and expressive in relationships," says lead researcher Wendy Troxel, an assistant professor of psychiatry and psychology. "After a bad night of sleep, women may be more likely to express irritability or frustration."[22]

> "I'm tired and get headaches all the time, which my doctor says is caused by my lack of sleep."[21]
>
> —Rebecca Wiseman, insomniac.

Bridget Davidson's sleep disorder destroyed her marriage. Davidson and her husband were very happy when they first married, but the stress of her job soon caused her to develop insomnia. This turned chronic, and she constantly felt exhausted. During the day she would snap at her husband and get irritated with him. After seven years, her husband was done. "John had told me that I had changed beyond recognition, that I was no longer the carefree, happy woman he'd met more than a decade earlier," Davidson recalls. "And, harsh though it was to hear, I could only agree."[23]

The Link to Heart Disease

Disrupted sleep from any sleep disorder can lead to significant health problems. Chronic insomnia, for example, can increase one's risk of heart problems. In 2013 the *European Heart Journal* published a study

Laughing with Narcolepsy

Jimmy Kimmel is best known for being a funny talk-show host. However, to those suffering from narcolepsy, he is an inspiration. Kimmel rose to stardom despite being a narcoleptic. He began suffering from the symptoms of sleep attacks in his early adulthood. "I would get very tired for no reason," he says. "I would doze off in meetings, watching TV, even driving." He finally decided to see a doctor. Once diagnosed, he was prescribed a medication to help with the symptoms, and Kimmel decided he would not let narcolepsy get in his way. In fact, he even jokes about it during his interviews. "I've never used my narcolepsy in my work, though I do have a dream to someday use up an entire hour of television time by sleeping."

Jimmy Kimmel, as told to Brendan Vaughan, "What It Feels Like to Have Narcolepsy," JimmyKimmel.net. http://jimmykimmel.net.

that linked chronic insomnia and heart issues. The study gathered data on 54,279 Norwegian adults who had difficulty falling asleep, difficulty staying asleep, and woke up feeling weary. None of the participants had heart disease at the start of the study, but after an average eleven-year follow-up period, there were 1,412 cases of heart failure. The researchers concluded that a person with one symptom of insomnia had a 17 percent increased risk of developing heart failure compared to those without insomnia. Two symptoms of insomnia increased the chances by 92 percent, and three increased a person's chances by almost 300 percent.

Heart issues are also associated with sleep apnea. An estimated thirty-eight thousand cardiovascular deaths occur each year due to untreated sleep apnea. A person with sleep apnea does not get enough oxygen because his or her breathing repeatedly stops during sleep, which can result in heart attacks and strokes.

Obesity, Diabetes—Even Death

Lack of sleep also puts people at greater risk of becoming obese and developing diabetes, according to a study published in a 2012 issue of *Science Translational Medicine*. Both sporadic and irregular sleep may decrease a person's metabolic rate, which could contribute to weight gain. The study included twenty-one healthy people who underwent sleep-cycle tests for six weeks. The researchers controlled how many hours of sleep each participant got and when they slept. They also varied the participants' sleep patterns. After a period of optimal sleep, or ten hours, study participants were only allowed to sleep about six hours in a twenty-four-hour period.

Researchers found that the insulin response of the pancreas—in which the pancreas releases insulin to regulate the body's blood sugar after a meal—was lower in a person who had received inadequate sleep. Because of a slower response, the person's glucose level (the amount of sugar in the blood) rose higher and for longer after a meal, and his or her resting metabolic rate (the rate at which the body burns calories) decreased. When a person's blood sugar goes up and metabolic rates go down, he or she is at greater risk of developing obesity and diabetes.

"Lack of sleep for a long enough time can cause depression."[24]

—Prashant Gajwani, associate professor of psychiatry and behavioral sciences.

An even more dangerous consequence of not getting enough sleep is an increased mortality risk. Indeed, a 2010 Penn State study found that lack of sleep can be fatal. In the study 1,741 people were observed in a sleep laboratory and were checked on periodically for more than a decade. The study found that men with insomnia who slept less than six hours per day were four times more likely to die than those who got a full night's rest on a regular basis.

Sleep Disorders and Depression

Physical ailments are not the only long-term health issues; depression also goes hand in hand with having a sleep disorder. In some cases sleep disorders are a factor in developing depression, but in others depression causes sleep disorders. "Lack of sleep for a long enough time can cause depression,"[24] says Prashant Gajwani, an associate professor of psychiatry and behavioral sciences at the University of Texas Medical School.

Sleep apnea has been specifically linked to depression. In 2012 researchers at the Centers for Disease Control and Prevention found that men diagnosed with sleep apnea were more than twice as likely as other men to show symptoms of clinical depression. These symptoms included feeling hopeless and uninterested in everyday activities. Women with sleep apnea were five times more likely to be at risk for depression.

Depression is very common in individuals who experience sleep disorders. People with sleep apnea or insomnia, for example, are statistically more likely to exhibit signs of clinical depression than those who get a more restful sleep.

A person with insomnia has an even greater risk of developing depression. A 2005 study reported in the US National Library of Medicine found that insomniacs were ten times as likely to have depression as those without insomnia, and they were seventeen times more likely to experience anxiety. Supporting these findings was the National Sleep Foundation's 2006 Sleep in America poll, which focused on children aged eleven to seventeen. The survey found a strong association between negative mood and sleep problems. Among adolescents who reported being unhappy, 73 percent reported not sleeping enough at night.

Karen Lange has dealt with depression and anxiety for more than a decade. She also battles insomnia and feels tired many days. She believes that depression and sleep anxiety are linked. "I think not getting enough sleep made my depression worse," Lange says. "I'd wake up not rested and would feel worse about the general state of life."[25]

Pain and Danger Among the Effects

Suddenly falling asleep while talking to someone, having shooting pains down your legs, or hurting yourself while sleeping are other problems that people with sleep disorders must deal with on a daily basis.

People with narcolepsy must take particular caution as they go through life, since they might fall asleep at any moment. Falling asleep while driving or walking around in a public place can be extremely dangerous, and they can hurt themselves or others. Many with narcolepsy have learned to recognize certain signs of impending sleep, such as feeling disoriented and sluggish, although they do not have much time to ready themselves.

Julie Flygare has accepted her narcoleptic attacks as a normal part of her life and has crafted methods for dealing with them. "When I sense sleep lurking behind me, even in the far distance, I start preparing for its arrival. If I'm driving, I pull over to the best possible spot," writes Flygare. "If I'm out in public, I try to reach a bathroom or semi-private space. Lying down is ideal, but sitting with my head supported works too."[26]

Restless legs syndrome (RLS) sufferers have their own set of issues. In addition to dealing with sleep deprivation, they also suffer leg pains. Joyce Bocek has experienced RLS for about thirty years. Initially the throbbing and shooting pains just occurred at night. Increasingly, though, the spasms began to occur during the day. "The smallest things can trigger an RLS episode," writes Bocek. "My cat brushing against my leg, a pedicurist touching my foot, an itch on my thigh."[27]

RBD also has its own unique problems. While sleeping, sufferers need to ensure they are in a safe place in case they begin acting out their dreams. During their REM sleep, those with this disorder have been known to fall out of bed, cut themselves, trip while walking, and hurt the people near them. Many have learned to take precautions, such as placing something beside their bed so they do not fall out or surrounding themselves with pillows to restrict movement and reduce the chance of hurting themselves or others.

> "When I sense sleep lurking behind me, even in the far distance, I start preparing for its arrival. If I'm driving, I pull over to the best possible spot."[26]
>
> —Julie Flygare, narcoleptic.

Coping with a Sleep Disorder

Living with sleep disorders is difficult, but many learn to cope. Ruth Carter has dealt with insomnia on and off for her whole adult life, and she tries not to feel anxiety over it. "One thing I've learned about insomnia is not to freak out about it," writes Carter. "When you freak out about your insomnia, you make yourself anxious which makes the insomnia worse and it becomes a self-perpetuating cycle."[28]

Another way people deal with sleeplessness is to make the rest of their lives as healthy as possible. Both physical activity and a healthy diet can help the body combat the effects of sleep deprivation. Being physically active and eating nutritiously will help sleep-deprived individuals feel better during the day and may even help them sleep better.

Many complain that it makes them feel lonely to be awake while others sleep. Finding ways to be productive and communicative at night is thus a helpful coping strategy. A.L. Kennedy, an insomniac, spends her long nights reading, watching shows, and e-mailing friends as opposed to lying in bed hoping for sleep. "The loneliness [insomnia] seems to create in its particular dark can be alleviated," writes Kennedy. "Books are wonderful company and the Internet puts people in other time zones within reach."[29]

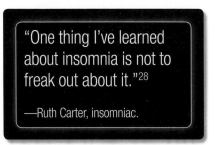

"One thing I've learned about insomnia is not to freak out about it."[28]

—Ruth Carter, insomniac.

Others have found that listening to talk radio disrupts their anxious thoughts and worries and at times will even lull them to sleep. Another coping mechanism is to use the sleeplessness as a creative inspiration, writing down thoughts, stories, and ideas. Like Kennedy, there are millions of people who know that life with a sleep disorder is not easy, and sufferers find they must be resilient to cope.

CHAPTER 4

Can Sleep Disorders Be Treated?

Each year sleep disorders, sleep deprivation, and sleepiness add an estimated $15.9 billion to the national health care bill, according to the National Center on Sleep Disorders Research. Tied to this are lost worker productivity and expensive accidents. For this reason, the US government has invested millions in researching sleep disorder treatments. At the National Institutes of Health, the amount budgeted for sleep research in 2015 was $235 million. The hope is that this research will yield more treatments for millions of Americans.

Doctors and researchers have not yet developed a cure for any sleep disorder. However, with treatment, most sleep disorders are manageable, and people can completely recover from certain ones, such as acute insomnia. Others, like narcolepsy and restless legs syndrome (RLS), are lifelong conditions but can still be treated to alleviate their symptoms. There are several ways to treat sleep disorders, but their success varies due to circumstances and individuals.

Treating Insomnia

After a diagnosis, the first step is to determine whether the insomnia is the result of a medical condition such as depression, diabetes, or kidney disease. Additionally, doctors will evaluate any medications the person is on because certain drugs, such as corticosteroids for asthma, can cause insomnia. If the insomnia is caused by any of these factors, it can be quite treatable. Treating the underlying medical condition or changing the problematic medication typically makes the insomnia go away.

Other treatments are used when the insomnia is caused by stress or life changes or when the cause remains unknown. One treatment involves diet. Doctors suggest insomniacs should eliminate caffeine, alcohol, and nicotine because these can contribute to wakefulness. Doctors also recommend that people should exercise, but not within two hours of bedtime because physical activity can stimulate the brain and heart and keep a person awake. Another suggestion is to avoid electronics and any kind of screen time before bed. Some sleep researchers have found that exposure to light-emitting electronics can disturb sleep patterns and worsen insomnia. According to Phyllis Zee, the director of Northwestern University's Center for Sleep & Circadian Biology, the light from a tablet or laptop can be "sufficiently stimulating to the brain to make it more awake and delay your ability to sleep."[30]

Instituting good sleep hygiene—a term for bedtime behaviors—can also reduce insomnia. Making bedtime a quiet, relaxing time, darkening the room, using a sleep mask, and wearing earplugs to eliminate outside stimulation have been shown to improve the ability to fall asleep. Sleep professionals also emphasize that beds are meant for sleeping. If a person wakes up in the middle of the night and is awake for more than fifteen minutes, he or she should get out of bed, go do something else, and then come back to bed. Professionals state that lying in bed awake for extended periods of time may encourage a person to associate his or her bed with sleep deprivation.

Sleeping Pills

An estimated 40 million or more Americans regularly use over-the-counter or prescription sleeping pills. In fact, according to IMS Health, which tracks pharmaceutical sales, Americans spend about $2 billion per year on prescription sleep drugs. Doctors recommend these pharmaceutical sleep aids when other treatments do not work.

Over-the-counter sleep aids can help with minor cases of insomnia. Most contain antihistamines, the same ingredient found in many allergy medicines, and promote drowsiness. However, they cannot be taken for more than a few days, as tolerance to the antihistamines' ef-

Sleeping Pill Use Increases with Age

Sleeping pill use dramatically increases with age, probably because sleep disorders are more likely to affect people as they get older. In general, physical changes and medications make it more difficult for older people to sleep.

Percentage of adults aged 20 and over who used prescription sleep aids in the past 30 days, by age: United States, 2005–2010

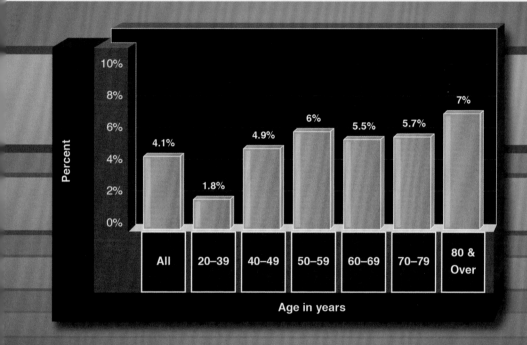

Source: Centers for Disease Control and Prevention, "Prescription Sleep Aid Use Among Adults, United States, 2005–2010," August 2013. www.cdc.gov.

fects can develop quickly; this means that the longer the drug is taken, the less effective it becomes. These drugs also have inhibiting side effects, such as daytime grogginess.

Prescription sleep aids are also available, and a doctor will typically prescribe these in cases where behavioral changes have not worked. Drugs will not cure any underlying issues causing insomnia, but they may provide temporary relief. There are two main types of prescription drugs—benzodiazepines and Z-drugs. Benzodiazepines, which are tranquilizers that include Valium, are a group of medicines that slow down the nervous system and produce sedation and relaxation. They are not used as often as they once were due to their side effects, which include dizziness, blurred vision, and daytime drowsiness.

Ambien, Lunesta, and Sonata are popular brands of Z-drugs, sleeping pills that are more common today. These work by mimicking the action of gamma-aminobutyric acid (GABA), which is an inhibitory neurotransmitter that induces sleepiness. All Z-drugs have side effects, including dizziness, daytime memory loss, daytime grogginess, gastrointestinal problems, and potential addiction. Ambien also has been associated with blackouts in which the person wakes up but is not aware of his or her actions. In extreme cases, particularly when Ambien has been mixed with alcohol, people have put themselves and others in serious danger. In 2008, for example, Julie Ann Bronson drank several glasses of wine, took two Ambien pills, and went to bed. She later woke up but remained in a blackout state. Bronson got in her car and started driving while still barefoot and in pajamas. She ran over a mother and her two daughters, all of whom survived but suffered injuries. Because of these side effects, doctors only recommend using sleeping pills for short periods of time, when sleep is absolutely necessary and no other method is working.

Spray Yourself to Sleep

The latest innovation in sleep solutions involves a spritz. Sprayable Sleep is a melatonin-based topical sleep-aid spray. This spray is applied directly to the skin to deliver a low dose of melatonin, a hormone that helps regulate sleep. The product has about 0.25 milligrams of melatonin per spritz, and one bottle has enough for one month of use. Producers of this spray claim it works better than a melatonin pill because it has a lower level of melatonin that helps people feel less groggy upon waking.

Many are hoping that a new class of sleep aid will help people sleep without the side effects. Orexin antagonists were approved by the US Food and Drug Administration in 2014. Unlike current Z-drugs, which promote GABA to shut down the brain, orexin antagonists block orexins, which are brain chemicals that promote wakefulness. These aids are supposed to induce sleep without causing daytime drowsiness or grogginess. Belsomra, produced by Merck, is one of the first such drugs to be sold to the public.

The effectiveness of sleeping pills often depends on the person. Some find them extremely helpful to overcome bouts of insomnia. Others find that they must continually take the drug in order for it to work. Laurie Sandell experienced this after taking Ambien to deal with her chronic and severe insomnia. "Before long I needed to take a pill every night," writes Sandell. "If I tried to fall asleep naturally, I would have what's called 'rebound insomnia,' meaning I would be up all night as a result of taking the drug the night before."[31] Sandell's use of Ambien led to an addiction, another risk of such medications.

Is Melatonin Better?

Another way people treat sleep issues is to take synthetic melatonin. Melatonin is a natural hormone made by the body's pineal gland, which is located just above the middle of the brain. The pineal is inactive during the day, but it becomes active around 9:00 p.m. and produces melatonin, which is released into the blood. Melatonin rises sharply, and people feel less alert and ready to sleep.

Melatonin supplements raise a person's melatonin levels beyond their natural amounts. Some people claim they prefer melatonin to sleeping pills because of its natural origins. People who have circadian rhythm disorders tend to benefit more from melatonin because it is linked to the internal clock, which is the source of their problems. Melatonin supplements help some correctly adjust to day and night. Melatonin is also often used by travelers to overcome jet lag–related insomnia.

Cognitive Behavioral Therapy

Many health professionals believe the best way to treat chronic insomnia is with cognitive behavioral therapy (CBT). This is because

CBT's purpose is to effect long-term changes in a person's relationship with sleep—to solve the underlying cause of a sleep problem so he or she will not need pills or other remedies. CBT is a structured program that identifies and replaces thoughts and behaviors that cause sleep problems with habits that promote restful sleep.

The program includes several treatment components. Patients initially have their sleep reduced to only five hours per night. This is intended to increase their need for sleep. After several days, experts

Mental health professionals believe cognitive behavioral therapy (CBT) can be an effective treatment for patients with sleep disorders. CBT teaches patients to train their bodies and minds to respond to relaxation techniques and avoid anxiety-filled practices that might aggravate their specific disorder.

believe a person's sleep needs are reset. Because the body craves sleep, the patient can be trained to develop normal sleep habits. The program also eliminates time spent in bed while awake to reduce the association between being in bed and feeling anxious about not being able to fall asleep. The patient also attends therapy sessions to learn how to replace negative sleep-related behaviors with relaxation techniques.

There are a variety of CBT programs specific to insomnia offered throughout the country. An example is a four-week program offered by the Cleveland Clinic. The first week focuses on sleep/lifestyle habits, the second on sleep education and relaxation training, the third on cognitive therapy, and the fourth on relapse prevention.

CBT takes a lot of time and effort, though many say the efforts are worth it. Bruce Rybarczyk, a clinical psychologist at Virginia Commonwealth University, offers intense CBT treatment that teaches a person how to sleep. "I often refer to CBT-I [cognitive behavioral therapy for insomnia] as sleep boot camp," says Rybarczyk. "Essentially, through CBT we want to retrain the sleep process and provide the patient with an owner's manual for their sleep system by educating them about the science of sleep."[32]

> "We want to retrain the sleep process and provide the patient with an owner's manual for their sleep system."[32]
>
> —Bruce Rybarczyk, clinical psychologist at Virginia Commonwealth University.

CBT appears to have positive results. In one study, sixty-three insomnia sufferers were randomly assigned to one of four treatments: CBT, Ambien, CBT plus Ambien, or a placebo (a substance that has no effects). The CBT consisted of four thirty-minute sessions (once weekly for three weeks, then a final session two weeks later), plus a fifteen-minute follow-up phone call. Nearly 60 percent of the CBT-treated patients got to sleep as quickly as did people without insomnia, in thirty minutes or less. Even the CBT-treated patients who did not achieve normal sleep patterns got to sleep faster than they did before treatment. Most of them were falling asleep in forty-five minutes as opposed to an hour and a half, the average before sleep treatment.

Treating Other Disorders

Since many sleep disorders have the same symptoms as insomnia, insomnia treatments are useful for addressing other sleep disorders. However, many sleep disorders also have their own treatments.

Sleep apnea sufferers, for example, can lose weight to decrease their symptoms or even cure their problem. This is because overweight people have extra tissue in the back of their throats that can cover the airway and block the flow of air into the lungs while they sleep. Losing weight can reduce the extra tissue and open up the passage. "If we can get people to lose weight, it would make both sleep apnea and other health problems . . . go away,"[33] says Lawrence Epstein, the assistant medical director of clinical sleep medicine at Brigham and Women's Hospital. According to Epstein, losing just 10 percent of one's body weight can reduce sleep apnea symptoms, and losing a significant amount of weight can even cure the condition.

> "If we can get people to lose weight, it would make both sleep apnea and other health problems . . . go away."[33]
>
> —Lawrence Epstein, assistant medical director of clinical sleep medicine at Brigham and Women's Hospital.

Another treatment for sleep apnea is to use continuous positive airway pressure (CPAP) while sleeping. A CPAP mask or device fits over the nose and mouth and blows air into the airways to keep them open at night. Although CPAP devices are highly effective, many people have difficulty using them at night; some complain they are uncomfortable and clunky. One study estimated that 30 to 50 percent of CPAP users do not like their treatment, and another survey discovered that about half of CPAP patients stopped using their device within one to two weeks.

An alternative treatment for those with obstructive sleep apnea is mandibular advancement devices. These are mouthpieces that snap over the upper and lower dental arches and have metal hinges that make it possible for the lower jaw to be eased forward. This tightens the soft tissue and muscles of the upper airway to prevent its obstruction during sleep. Clinical studies have shown that these devices can be effective at treating mild to moderate sleep apnea.

In cases where CPAP devices fail to effect change, surgery can be an option. Uvulopalatopharyngoplasty is the most common sleep

A continuous positive airway pressure (CPAP) mask is the most commonly prescribed treatment to regulate breathing in patients who suffer from obstructive sleep apnea. However, many who have tried these masks find them too uncomfortable to use every night.

Cured with an App?

Insomniacs who do not want to take sleeping pills but also do not have time to attend cognitive behavior therapy sessions can turn to an app for help. Sleepio, available via its website, can now be downloaded onto Apple products; it was released for iOS 8 in 2014. It features an animated therapist, a personal sleep expert, and comes with a questionnaire to determine a specific sleep problem. The user keeps a sleep diary that the program uses to provide feedback.

The therapist provides a weekly lesson with step-by-step directions, such as how to set up a calm sleep environment and reduce negative thoughts. The goal is to reset the user's body on a course to healthier sleep. The app is based on the information in *Overcoming Insomnia and Sleep Problems* by Colin Espie, a professor at the University of Glasgow. Initial results of the app appear positive. A randomized trial found that after six weeks of use, Sleepio's web app helped 75 percent of people with persistent sleep problems improve their sleep.

apnea surgical procedure. It removes excess tissue from the soft palate and pharynx. Another surgery is the pillar procedure, a minimally invasive approach that involves placing three polyester rods into the soft palate, making it less likely to come into contact with the back wall of the pharynx. Nasal surgeries or removing the tonsils can also help sufferers of sleep apnea.

Let There Be Light

Circadian rhythm disorders have their own set of therapies. People with these disorders have internal clocks that do not work in time with a normal day and night schedule. Among other factors, the clock is "set" by exposure to bright light such as sunlight. Therefore, exposure to bright light, or light therapy, is one way to reset the internal clock. The most common light therapy involves plugging in a light box that gives off twenty-five hundred to five thousand lux (a measurement of the amount of light produced). The patient sits 18 to 24 inches (46 to 61 cm) away from the box for fifteen to thirty minutes once or twice a day.

Another method is chronotherapy, a behavioral technique used to change the sleep-wake cycle. The person's room must be pitch black at bedtime for this to work. If the patient tends to go to bed late (say, around 2:00 a.m.), he or she is instructed to gradually shift bedtime one to three hours forward each day until a more traditional bedtime is reached. For example, if the patient wants to establish an 11:00 p.m. bedtime, he or she would go to bed the next "night" at 5:00 a.m., the next night at 8:00 a.m., and continue this pattern until the desired bedtime of 11:00 p.m. is achieved.

The recent discovery of a protein called REV-ERB is furthering research into treatments for circadian rhythm disorders. REV-ERB plays a key role in regulating mammals' internal clocks. A 2014 study published in *Nature Communications* reported that REV-ERB directs the activity of circadian proteins. Researchers found that giving mice a synthetic compound that turned on REV-ERB altered their circadian rhythm. Better understanding REV-ERB's role in the body could lead to the development of drugs to treat circadian problems.

Stopping the Throbbing

Sufferers of RLS cannot sleep because their legs throb and they feel the need to move. Treating RLS can sometimes be easy. If the underlying problem is an iron deficiency, diabetes, or a drug reaction, treatment can be as simple as addressing that problem.

People whose RLS is not caused by these factors have a few different options. One is physical therapy, which includes stretching and massaging the affected areas. Exercise is also recommended, as is taking hot and cold baths to relax the muscles. These techniques have worked for Cherise Udell, who first experienced RLS when pregnant with her first daughter. Before bedtime, Udell takes a hot shower and does leg lunges. She also uses a medicated rub to ease the throbbing sensations. "I rub a generous amount of the menthol cream/ointment on my legs and jump into bed," she says. "Relief is immediate and within minutes I am joyfully asleep—no counting sheep required!"[34] Avoiding caffeine, nicotine, and alcohol are other ways to alleviate the symptoms associated with RLS.

> "I rub a generous amount of the menthol cream/ointment on my legs and jump into bed. Relief is immediate and within minutes I am joyfully asleep— no counting sheep required!"[34]
>
> —Cherise Udell, RLS sufferer.

Medication is usually recommended for people who experience RLS three or more nights a week. Such drugs do not cure RLS, but they relieve the symptoms. Medications include dopamine agonists, including pramipexole and rotigotine, which imitate the neurotransmitter dopamine in the brain. Because RLS is related to a dysfunction in how dopamine is released, these drugs are used to increase the patient's level of dopamine. They have been found to relieve the leg throbbing, allowing for sleep.

Adapting to Narcolepsy

Narcoleptics do not have problems falling asleep; rather, they are unable to control *when* they fall asleep. There is no cure for narcolepsy, but several lifestyle adaptations and drugs can treat narcolepsy's various symptoms. For narcoleptics with milder symptoms, doctors recommend taking three or more scheduled naps throughout the day to counteract excessive sleepiness and unplanned sleep. Additionally, patients should also avoid eating heavy meals and drinking alcohol, which can interfere with sleep.

Much research regarding narcolepsy is being conducted at Stanford University's Center for Narcolepsy. Today's drug treatments only address narcolepsy's symptoms and not its cause, so researchers are trying to fix that. Specifically, researchers are working to develop drugs that can stimulate the hypocretin receptors in order to replace the depleted hypocretins in narcoleptics. This is not an easy task, however. Hypocretins are unstable and need to be broken down before reaching the brain; developing a drug that accomplishes this is challenging.

In the meantime, narcoleptics with more severe symptoms may be prescribed drugs to help them stay awake during the day. Doctors often prescribe stimulants such as modafinil (Provigil) or armodafinil (Nuvigil) because these are not very addictive and do not produce the mood highs and lows often associated with other stimulants. Other drugs used to treat narcolepsy include selective serotonin reuptake inhibitors or serotonin and norepinephrine reuptake inhibitors, which are used to suppress REM sleep and alleviate cataplexy (loss of muscle control), hallucinations, and sleep paralysis.

Such treatments have helped narcoleptics live normal, successful lives. For example, Todd was just fifteen when he developed narcolepsy and cataplexy. Because he was diagnosed early, his treatment allowed him to finish high school, attend college, and build a successful career. "My medication lets me sleep at night, drive and be productive," he reports. The downside of such medications is that they can be quite expensive. Todd says he is very fortunate to have insurance. "If I didn't," he says, "the annual cost of Xyrem alone would be more than I earned last year."[35]

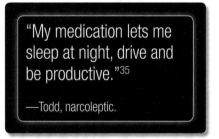

"My medication lets me sleep at night, drive and be productive."[35]

—Todd, narcoleptic.

Just Dreaming

Although no cure exists for REM behavior disorder (RBD), its symptoms can be treated. The main goal of treatment is to protect the patient and anyone nearby when he or she is sleeping. To this end, RBD sufferers have adopted protective measures at bedtime. They often move furniture and other items away from the bed so they cannot run into or use them, and they ensure that windows are closed and locked. Others have tried sleeping inside a sleeping bag to constrict their movements.

The purpose of RBD treatment is to allow the person to dream without acting out his or her dreams. The main way to treat this disorder is with medication, and the drug clonazepam is often prescribed. Taking it either significantly reduces or even completely curtails the problem, though its side effects may include daytime sleepiness and decreased balance.

With many different kinds of sleep research under way, scientists inch closer to finding more effective treatments and even cures. With the proper diagnosis, millions of Americans with sleep disorders have a good chance of regaining normal sleep patterns and getting much-needed rest.

SOURCE NOTES

Introduction: Everyone Needs Sleep

1. Cat Mocha, "My Story with Non-24," Circadian Sleep Disorders Network, November 24, 2014. www.circadiansleepdisorders.org.

2. Quoted in NPR, "Can't Sleep? Neither Can 60 Million Other Americans," May 20, 2008. www.npr.org.

3. Quoted in Jennifer Warner, "Poor Sleep May Raise Blood Pressure," WebMD, August 29, 2011. www.webmd.com.

4. Quoted in Judith Graham, "Sleep Disorders a Nightmare for Many," *Chicago Tribune*, April 6, 2010. http://articles.chicagotribune.com.

Chapter 1: What Are Sleep Disorders?

5. Cleveland Clinic, "Common Sleep Disorders," 2014. http://my.clevelandclinic.org.

6. Quoted in American Sleep Apnea Association, "Bob's Story," 2015. www.sleepapnea.org.

7. Seth Maxon, "How Sleep Deprivation Decays the Mind and Body," *Atlantic*, December 2013. www.theatlantic.com.

8. Dominie Soo Bush, "Dominie's Insomnia Story," Dominie's Fibromyalgia and Chronic Fatigue Syndrome Homepage. www.fms-help.com.

9. Linda Ledingham, "Living with Restless Leg Syndrome," Just in Time Wellness, 2010. www.justintimewellness.com.

10. Amanda Vasas, "Amanda's Story," Narcolepsy Network, 2015. http://narcolepsynetwork.org.

11. Oijo Baphuacs, *The Sandman Is from Mars: Defeating the Non-24hr Sleep-Wake Syndrome* (blog), September 27, 2009. http://non24.blogspot.com.

Chapter 2: What Causes Sleep Disorders?

12. Erin Fuchs, "I Spent 21 Hours Hooked Up to a Sleep Machine, and What I Learned Could Change My Life," Business Insider, January 14, 2015. www.businessinsider.com.

13. Neil B. Kavey, "Stress and Insomnia," National Sleep Foundation. http://sleepfoundation.org.

14. Quoted in Hub, "Insomniac's Brain 'Like a Light Switch That Is Always On,' Hopkins Researcher Says," February 28, 2014. http://hub.jhu.edu.

15. Quoted in Philly.com, "Tongue Fat May Be Key in Treating Sleep Apnea," October 2, 2014. http://articles.philly.com.

16. Quoted in PR Newswire, "While Asleep, People Act Out Their Dreams," December 18, 2012. www.prnewswire.com.

Chapter 3: What Is It Like to Live with a Sleep Disorder?

17. Quoted in Lawrence Health Center, "How Much Sleep Do People Really Need?," October 17, 2014. www.lawrencehealthcenter.com.

18. Quoted in ABC News, "Sleepy Drivers Can Be Deadly," April 23, 2007. http://abcnews.go.com.

19. Quoted in Param Kumar, "A Good Night of Sleep Can Improve Memory and Learning," Westside Story, June 7, 2014. http://thewestsidestory.net.

20. Quoted in Gail Belsky, "What Insomnia Feels Like: You're Always Tired, but Not Sleepy," Health.com, April 26, 2008. www.health.com.

21. Quoted in Health.com, "Insomnia's Emotional Toll: A Young Mom Shares Her Struggle with Sleep and Stress," April 21, 2008. www.health.com.

22. Quoted in Ella Quittner, "Sleep Problems May Fuel Marital Discord," CNN, June 14, 2011. www.cnn.com.

23. Quoted in Lorraine Fisher, "'Insomnia Destroyed My Marriage': One Woman's Account of How Sleepless Nights Robbed Her of a Husband," *Daily Mail* (London), May 6, 2011. www.dailymail .co.uk.

24. Quoted Chris Iliades, "Depression and Sleep: Getting the Right Amount," Everyday Health, September 14, 2012. www.everyday health.com.

25. Quoted in Office on Women's Health, "An Interview with a Woman Overcoming Depression and Anxiety: Karen Lange," September 4, 2013. http://womenshealth.gov.

26. Julie Flygare, "Sleep's Choice: Living with Narcolepsy," Sleep Foundation, October 12, 2012. http://sleepfoundation.org.

27. Joyce Bocek, "Living with Restless Legs Syndrome," InfoBarrel, August 22, 2014. www.infobarrel.com.

28. Ruth Carter, "Living with Insomnia," *Undeniable Ruth* (blog), July 23, 2013. www.undeniableruth.com.

29. A.L. Kennedy, "Insomnia and Me: A.L. Kennedy," *Guardian* (Manchester, UK), April 19, 2014. www.theguardian.com.

Chapter 4: Can Sleep Disorders Be Treated?

30. Quoted in John Sutter, "Trouble Sleeping? Maybe It's Your iPad," CNN, May 13, 2010. www.cnn.com.

31. Laurie Sandell, "Diary of a Sleeping Pill Junkie," *Glamour*, March 2008. www.glamour.com.

32. Quoted in Sathya Achia Abraham, "Sleep Boot Camp: A Wake Up Call for Insomnia Sufferers," VCU Across the Spectrum, February 24, 2014. www.spectrum.vcu.edu.

33. Quoted in Stephanie Watson, "Weight Loss, Breathing Devices Still Best for Treating Obstructive Sleep Apnea," *Harvard Health Blog*, Harvard Medical School, October 2, 2013. www.health .harvard.edu.

34. Cherise Udell, "4 Home Remedies for Restless Legs," Care 2, June 24, 2013. www.care2.com.

35. Quoted in OHSU Brain Institute, "Todd's Story." www.ohsu.edu.

ORGANIZATIONS TO CONTACT

American Academy of Sleep Medicine
2510 N. Frontage Rd.
Darien, IL 60561
phone: (630) 737-9700
website: www.aasmnet.org

The American Academy of Sleep Medicine is dedicated to improving sleep health. It does this by providing sleep medicine advocacy, education, strategic research, and practice standards.

American Sleep Apnea Association
1717 Pennsylvania Ave. NW, Suite 1025
Washington, DC 20006
phone: (888) 293-3650
website: www.sleepapnea.org

This organization provides information for those afflicted with sleep apnea and advocates for research and policies to help those with the disorder.

American Sleep Association
1002 Lititz Pike #229
Lititz, PA 17543
www.sleepassociation.org

This nonprofit organization is dedicated to providing public awareness about sleep disorders and sleep health. It also promotes sleep medicine research, and communication between patients, physicians, healthcare professionals, corporations, and scientists.

Circadian Sleep Disorders Network
website: www.circadiansleepdisorders.org

This is an all-volunteer organization that provides health and treatment information to those afflicted with circadian sleep disorders. It advocates for research and treatment options for these disorders.

International Parkinson and Movement Disorder Society

555 E. Wells Street, Suite 1100
Milwaukee, WI 53202
Phone: (414) 276-2145
www.movementdisorders.org

This is a professional society of clinicians, scientists, and other health-care professionals who are interested in Parkinson's disease, and related neurodegenerative and neurodevelopmental disorders, including restless legs syndrome. Their goal is to advance research in all areas of these disorders.

Johns Hopkins Center for Restless Legs Syndrome

Johns Hopkins Sleep Disorders Center
Allergy & Asthma Center, 4th Floor
5501 Hopkins Bayview Circle
Baltimore, MD 21224
phone: (410) 550-0571
website: www.hopkinsmedicine.org

This organization conducts and supports research, and hosts conferences on restless legs syndrome. It also provides patients with information about the causes, diagnosis, prevention, and treatment of the syndrome.

Narcolepsy Network

129 Waterwheel Ln.
North Kingstown, RI 02852
phone: (888) 292-6522
website: http://narcolepsynetwork.org

The Narcolepsy Network is a nonprofit organization that provides resources and information about narcolepsy to narcoleptics and their families. It helps in the formation of support groups for those with narcolepsy, and it helps provide public awareness.

National Institutes of Health

9000 Rockville Pike
Bethesda, MD 20892
phone: (301) 496-4000
website: www.nih.gov

The National Institutes of Health is a government organization dedicated to Americans' health. This institution funds medical research, including research into the causes and treatment of sleep disorders.

National Sleep Foundation

1010 N. Glebe Rd., Suite 310
Arlington, VA 22201
phone: (703) 243-1697
website: http://sleepfoundation.org

The National Sleep Foundation's focus is to improve health and well-being through sleep education and advocacy. It provides information about the causes, risks, and treatments for the many types of sleep disorders.

Sleep, Metabolism and Health Center

5841 S. Maryland, MC1027
Chicago, IL 60637
http://sleep.uchicago.edu

This is the University of Chicago's sleep research center. Established in 2010, it is nationally and internationally recognized as a leading institution for sleep research.

The Stanford Center for Sleep Sciences and Medicine

3165 Porter Dr., MC 5480
Palo Alto, CA 94304
phone: (650) 723-6601
website: http://sleep.stanford.edu

This center was established to conduct research and provide clinical and educational programs to advance the field of sleep medicine and improve patient care. The center was founded in the 1970s and has made many important contributions to the field since that time.

FOR FURTHER RESEARCH

Books

Atlantic Publishing, *How to Finally Wake Up Fresh and Naturally Energized: No More Sleepless Nights for You!* Ocala, FL: Atlantic, 2015.

Julie Flygare, *Wide Awake Dreaming*. Arlington, VA: Mill Pond Swan, 2012.

Himender Makker, *Sleep Medicine*. Oxford: Oxford University Press, 2015.

Steven Park, *Sleep, Interrupted: A Physician Reveals the #1 Reason Why So Many of Us Are Sick and Tired*. New York: Jodev, 2012.

David Randall, *Dreamland: Adventures in the Strange Science of Sleep*. New York: Norton, 2013.

Internet Sources

Jane Brody, "Hard Lesson in Sleep for Teenagers," *Well* (blog), NY Times.com, October 20, 2014. http://well.blogs.nytimes.com/2014/10/20/sleep-for-teenagers/.

John Cloud, "Has a Harvard Neurologist Discovered the Cure for Insomnia?," *New York*, December 4, 2014. http://nymag.com/daily/intelligencer/2014/12/will-a-new-discovery-help-cure-insomnia.html.

Madelyn Griffith-Haynie, "Jetlagged for Life," ADD-and-So-Much-More, October 9, 2012. http://addandsomuchmore.com/2012/10/09/jetlagged-for-life.

Johns Hopkins Medicine, "Causes of Restless Legs Syndrome." www.hopkinsmedicine.org/neurology_neurosurgery/centers_clinics/restless-legs-syndrome/what-is-rls/causes.html.

NPR, "Can't Sleep? Neither Can 60 Million Other Americans," May 20, 2008. www.npr.org/templates/story/story.php?storyId=906 38364.

Alice Park, "The Power of Sleep," *Time*, September 11, 2014. http://time.com/3326565/the-power-of-sleep.

U.S. News & World Report, "Why Do People Talk in Their Sleep?," March 11, 2015. www.yahoo.com/health/why-do-people-talk-in -their-sleep-113169728657.html.

Websites

Insomnia Blog (www.insomnialand.com/blog). This blog provides the latest information about insomnia and its health impacts and treatments.

Sleep Scholar (www.sleepscholar.com). This blog reports on current sleep medicine research and offers information about sleep industry–related projects.

Wake Up Narcolepsy (www.wakeupnarcolepsy.org/blog). This blog provides the latest in narcolepsy treatment, advocacy, and news.

INDEX

PICTURE CREDITS

ABOUT THE AUTHOR

Leanne Currie-McGhee has been happily writing educational books for over a decade. She resides in Norfolk, Virginia, with her husband and daughters, Grace and Hope.